DID YOU KNOW?
Platypus

young
reed

DID YOU KNOW?
Platypus

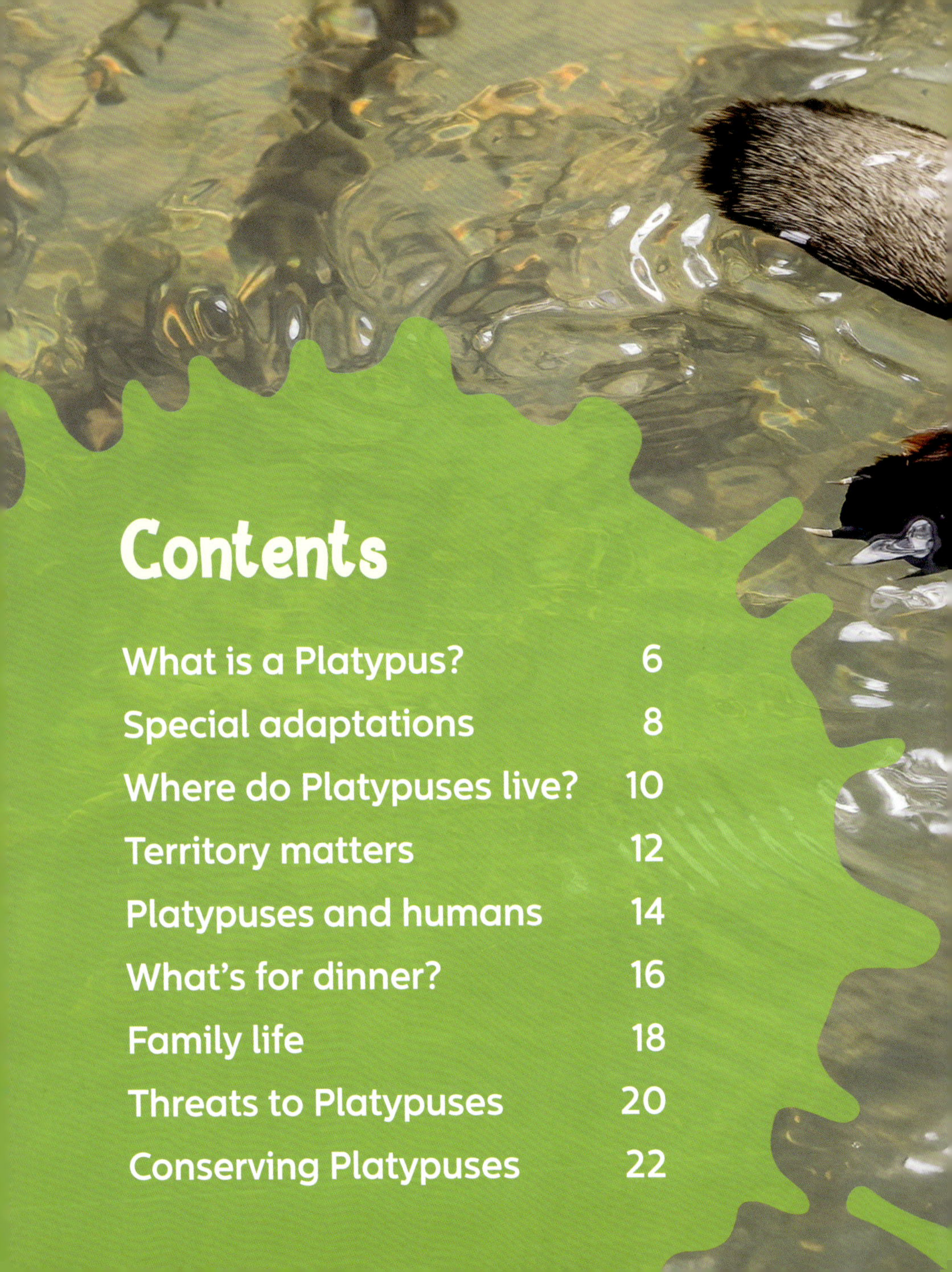

Contents

What is a Platypus? 6

Special adaptations 8

Where do Platypuses live? 10

Territory matters 12

Platypuses and humans 14

What's for dinner? 16

Family life 18

Threats to Platypuses 20

Conserving Platypuses 22

What is a Platypus?

- Platypuses are **mammals**, so they are **warm-blooded** and covered in fur. In Ancient Greek ***Platy*** means 'flat' and ***pus*** means 'foot', so the name translates as **'flat-foot'**.

- Measuring up to **sixty centimetres** in length and weighing up to **three kilograms**, they are specially adapted to **live and feed in wetlands** such as rivers and lakes.

- They belong to a family called the **monotremes**, which is very unusual for mammals in that the mum lays **eggs** rather than giving birth to babies.

- The only other animals in the monotreme family are the **Echidnas**, so although they look very different these spiny mammals are the Platypus's **closest relatives**.

Echidna.

Special adaptations

- Sometimes called the 'Duck-billed Platypus', its 'beak' is similar in appearance to a duck's but is **soft** in comparison.
- The texture of a Platypus bill feels more like skin. It is very sensitive and is able to **detect prey underwater.**
- To aid swimming underwater, these remarkable mammals also have a **paddle-like tail, sealable ears and nostrils, waterproof fur** and **webbed feet** (just like a duck).

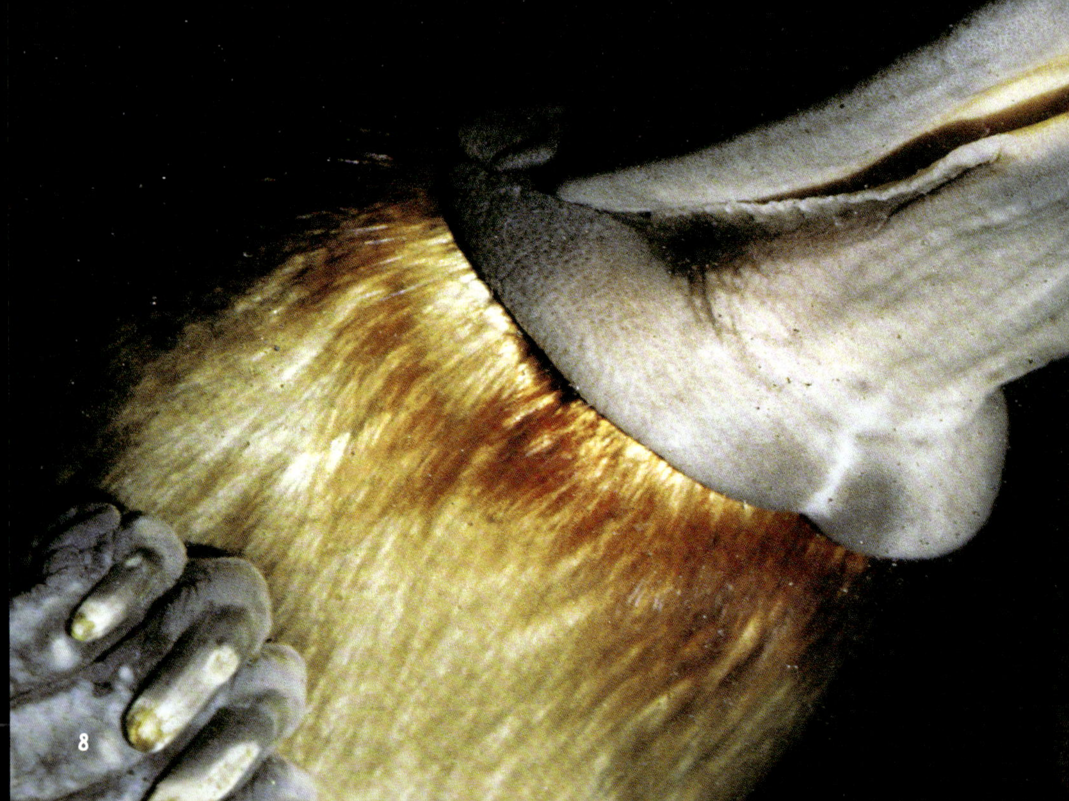

You can see how closely a duck's bill resembles that of a Platypus.

Where do Platypuses live?

- Platypuses are familiar around the world today thanks to TV documentaries and the fact that they are an iconic symbol of Australia

Wild Platypuses like to live in undisturbed rivers and streams.

- They can also be seen in some zoos and animal parks around Australia.
- In the wild, however, Platypuses live only in freshwater rivers, streams and lakes in eastern Australia, from Queensland to Tasmania.

Platypus in zoo.
(Wikimedia Commons)

Territory matters

- The area of a Platypus territory usually follows a stream or a river. It can extend from **two** to **seven kilometres** in length, depending on food availability, while males usually have bigger territories than females.

- A male Platypus has a **sharp claw** on its back leg that can **inject venom** into rivals while fighting for territory and mates. The venom is **extremely painful** for humans.

- When not swimming in the water, a Platypus will usually shelter **underground** in a burrow.

Webbed foot with poison spur.
(Wikimedia Commons)

Platypuses and humans

- They are such **strange animals** that the first European scientists to study Platypuses wondered whether they really existed or might have been made up as a **hoax.**

- Aboriginal people **hunted** Platypuses and depicted them in **artworks.** Today the species is known around the world as an **iconic symbol of Australia** that is celebrated in art and culture.

- Platypuses tend to be **shy** and are often **nocturnal,** being most active from dusk until dawn, so can be very difficult to see.

Look for ripples (left) when searching for a Platypus, and be sure not to confuse it with a Turtle (centre) or Water Rat (right).

● Your best chance of spotting one is to **visit a national park or nature reserve** where they are known to live. **Be very quiet**, so as not to disturb them, and **watch for ripples in the water**. But be careful not to confuse a Platypus with a Water Rat or Freshwater Turtle!

The Platypus is commonly depicted in artworks of all kinds, from sculpture to postage stamps.

What's for dinner?

- Platypuses hunt by diving **underwater** to catch small animals such as **insects** and their larvae, shrimps and worms, which they find on the bed of a river or stream.
- The Platypus has **no stomach**, so food passes straight to the intestines.

Aquatic larvae of insects such as Mayflies (above) and Damselflies (below) are good tucker for a Platypus.

• They also eat small stones, which they need to help them grind up their prey in their mouth, while food can be stored in their cheek pouches.

A Platypus often gives a little splash as it dives.

Family life

- Amazingly for a mammal, a female Platypus lays eggs rather than giving birth to babies. The eggs are about two centimetres long.
- A clutch of up to three eggs is laid in a leaf-lined nest in an underground chamber.

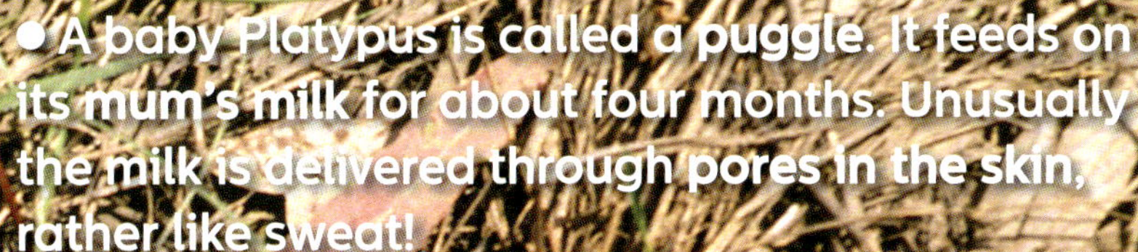

- A baby Platypus is called a puggle. It feeds on its mum's milk for about four months. Unusually the milk is delivered through pores in the skin, rather like sweat!
- Platypuses usually live alone, except during the breeding season and when the female is looking after the young.

The entrance to a Platypus burrow.

Platypus nest with two eggs.
(Wikimedia Commons)

Threats to Platypuses

- Most threats to the existence of Platypuses come from **humans**, including **habitat loss** due to developments such as buildings, roads, agriculture and dams.

Dingo.

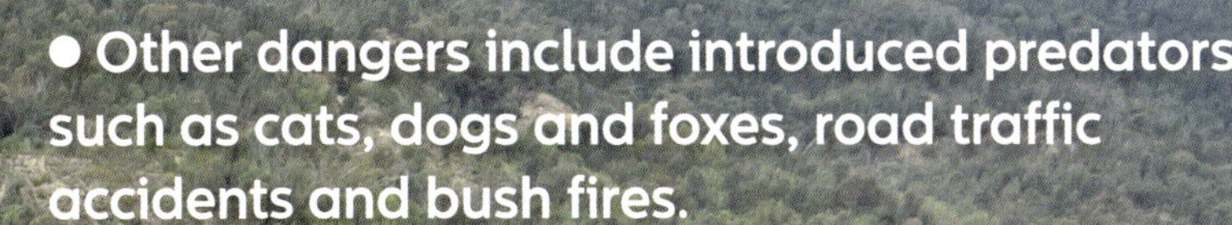

- Other dangers include introduced predators such as cats, dogs and foxes, road traffic accidents and bush fires.
- Dingos, monitor lizards, snakes and birds of prey are among the Platypus's natural predators.

Monitor lizard.

Dam projects and other human developments can lead to Platypus habitat loss.

Conserving Platypuses

- All of us need to do more to protect Platypus habitat, including keeping rivers clean, reducing disturbance, and keeping pet dogs away from places where Platypuses live.
- There are many kind people who help to conserve these amazing animals, including zoos that have set up captive-breeding programs to boost the population. There are also animal hospitals and rescue centres to help injured or orphaned Platypuses.

Ensuring that there are large areas of suitable habitat helps to maintain a healthy Platypus population.

There are many Platypus conservation projects in zoos and nature reserves around Australia.

First published in 2026 by Young Reed
– an imprint of Reed New Holland

newhollandpublishers.com

A record of this book is held at the National Library of Australia.

ISBN 9781760798161

Other titles in the '*Did You Know?*' series:

Capybara
ISBN 9781760798048

Crocodiles
ISBN 9781760798116

Dolphins
ISBN 9781760798000

Kangaroos
ISBN 9781921073861

Koala
ISBN 9781921073878

Lizards
ISBN 9781921073885

Meerkat
ISBN 9781921073892

Monkeys
ISBN 9781760798031

Penguins
ISBN 9781921073908

Platypus
ISBN 9781760798161

Quokka
ISBN 9781760798109

Red Panda
ISBN 9781921073915

Rhinos
ISBN 9781760798123

Sharks
ISBN 9781921078017

Tasmanian Devil
ISBN 9781760798055

Tigers
ISBN 9781760798024

Kea
ISBN 9781760798062

Kiwi
ISBN 9781760798079

For details of these books and hundreds of other Natural History titles see newhollandpublishers.com

And keep up with Reed New Holland and New Holland Publishers on Facebook and Instagram
ReedNewHolland and NewHollandPublishers @ReedNewHolland and @NewHollandPublishers

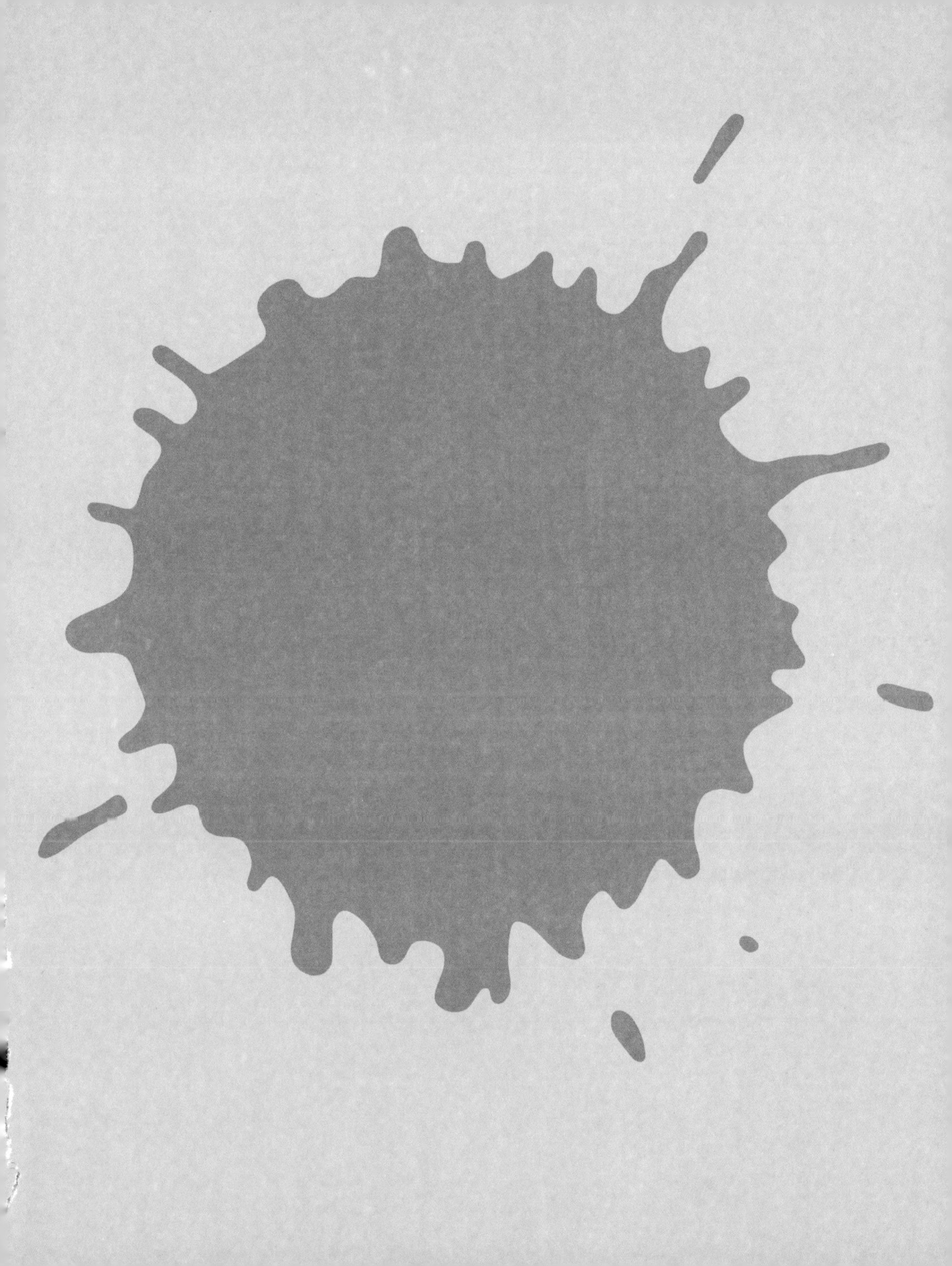